AF480965

Sparks Along the Warp

Sparks Along
the Warp

Suzanne Harris

Copyright © 2023 Suzanne Harris

Acknowledgements:

These poems have appeared in the following publications, some in slightly different form:

"Let Us Be Awake" first appeared in *Cascadia Daily News*, April 23, 2023 online edition.
"Solstice Prayer" first appeared in *Solstice—Light and Dark of the Salish Sea*, a poetry anthology, 2021.
"The Bear" won the *Sue C. Boynton Poetry Contest Walk Award*, 2020.
"Fork in the Road" first appeared in *Choices: 2016 Whatcom WRITES! Anthology.*

All rights reserved.

Published 2023
Printed in the United States of America
ISBN 979-8-8690-1823-6
Library of Congress Control Number: 202391268

CanyonWriter Press
1000 Harris #6
Bellingham, WA 98225
www.nancycanyon.com

Sparks Along the Warp

Cover Art: Nancy Canyon
Layout design: Suzanne Harris

For Steven

DAWN

MID-DAY

EVENING

DAWN

Let Us Be Awake

Let us be awake in the morning
before the sun has dried the fog,
undressed the trees.
When the divide between
sky, sea, and sand
is smudged—blurred
so that we know not if we walk
or swim or fly.
When the eternal
whisper and drumming waves
silence all else except
perhaps, the song of a gull;
and the waters scour
the sands to glass, clear and smooth
erasing the hieroglyphs
of night's receding tide—
let us be awake.

I See This Morning

Snow fell overnight.
Then skies cleared
bluing early morning light.
North wind promises
a week of cold.
The new year's frozen
before it's barely one day old.

Dawn

❖

Black as crows' wings
the night flees the sky
shadows struck stark
by the rising sun.

❖

Iridescent threads weave
sparks along the warp
of the great in-between,
cosmos inlays
cracklings of memory.

❖

Against the rising sun
I close my eyes
brightness black-red upon my lids.
I am Helios
racing his chariot forever
across the blue blue sky.

❖

Cool air on my skin
lingers—crisp, delicious,
long after I've come inside.
Invisible layer
conjoins me
to the world, transformed.

❖

Each new beginning
scrubs the early morning light—
summons our world
from the universal night.

Yesterday's Wind

scarred the snow
straight burrows
above the ground
exposing tips of grass
and sedge.
Savage motion frozen
in solemn morning light.

If I Were To Write a Song

Swept up by the reckless wind
rain batters my studio window.
Let it be a storm-song of praise.

Having hunkered against the chill,
endured the wet sting of cold
while darkness still held
its numbed but weakening grip
against the coming of the light,
I am self-satisfied to sing,
loving it all the better
for being warm and dry.

Line of Dawn

The line of dawn
slips around the earth,
an endless edge of transition.

Cacophony of junco
and chickadee rise each morning
as that line approaches.

Light—eight minutes
from the sun, cutting the horizon
like the prow of a ship.

Birdsong—continuous
rush of waves spilling
before the bow.

Thunder's Cry

At dawn, as I stand
on the wooden deck
massaging my thoughts
with gratitude for the coming day,
lightning scores the southeast sky
and moments later
I hear the thunder's cry.

First Light

I lie awake while primordial dawn
begins to chase away the brooding night
turning the absence of light
into this hazy gray.

Awake at the cusp of this fresh new hour
I listen to the robin and junco singing
their delicate heartbeats ringing
above the highest ray.

And now at last the sunshine rises
spreading out its effervescent glory
that never ending story
a love song to each day.

Solstice Prayer

Lauds in the garden while
a deep and sensuous blue
turns the night to dawn.
Skyline of trees a silhouette
without texture or line.
Flattened clouds slide
stealthily south to north
as black boughs shake
their leaves in the faint
wind's wake.

Geese orient to
magnetic sky lines,
chant their call to flight.
And now, the rooster
intones his blessing
on a new day—
Get up and watch its dawning!
Get up and sing its praise!

Spring, Not-Spring

Already bare branches shine
where the sun hoists itself
through a notch
in the hills,
just so.
The sky, still palest blue
hovers over
browns of winter
anxious
to be green, while
towhees and chickadees
zip between
woods and feeder
in anticipation.

Watching Venus

I wait and watch
bright Venus fade
into the azure sky.
Because I watch
so carefully
she does not pass me by.

Long after it seems
she should have fled
into the day's bright light
I track her still
through gauzy cloud—
faint beacon from the night.

Grammy

my grandmother stands
in the strawberry patch

next to the corn rows
that wave above her head

in the only picture
that bares her image

she was born in a logging camp
up Germany creek

when the trees were centurions
and the harvest eternal

she homesteaded the farm
and bore five children

who scattered when the war came
on the winds that drove the plow

she wanted to be an opera singer
before love and necessity bent

her to the land where she watched
her sons and daughter grow

into a world
breaking to be free

Entering By Way of Silence

This new day blooms
in softened colors
un-scrubbed by wind or storm.
Is there a pause
hanging in the air, a rest?

I move to open my window
enthralled by the pink underbellies
of variegated clouds, just in time
to see a vee of swans
winging eastward through
the tender colors of dawn.

Do they, too, blink and breathe
with wonder to be alive?

Pink Cheeks

Her cheeks flush
as she stands by the river's edge

chattering eagles
match the water's descending spiral

flashing blush of salmon
returning home.

Picking Cherries

Out in the orchard
deepening shades of red.
We approach with reverence.
Arms overhead
shoulders aching, fingertips numb,
tugging the firm fruit down
into our palms, into our mouths.

Triangular Vs punched into soft skin
from jays' first sampling,
causing fruit to wither, fermenting
just as they ripen. Weeks later,
crows caw drunkenly
dipping and turning overhead.

MID-DAY

In My House

Wood that grew elsewhere
now the framework and the finish.
Water straight from the ground
returns there, dribbling through the drain.

Breezes sometimes chase paper
from a desk, slam doors.
An afghan crocheted
by my grandmother, decades deceased.

Electricity waits to be spent,
and propane in the pipes—
ill-used but miraculous gift of dinosaurs.

Lettuce and cucumbers from the garden
this very morning,
while coffee beans and rice
have traveled more than me.

Multiple shades of blue and green
mix outdoor colors with inside hues.
And the sun, in its mid-day splendor
brightens all.

Searching For Consolation

Beside me on the table
the cactus blooms.
Outside my window,
trees shed their leaves,
tuck toward winter.
Returning chickadees and juncos
bob and flit,
grand parades of geese
honk overhead.

I tell myself
some rhythms still hold true,
hoping for consolation
in their recurring patterns.

There Is No Rhythm

There is no rhythm to the rain.
It gathers on the skylight,
drips through wooden slats,
splatters on the bricks.

Like the wind
tangled in trees,
or street water
shushed aside by tires,
like people
hunkered against the day,
or birds that have
all gone to ground,

my pen is ragged and disjointed,
mirroring the season
just now arriving.

The Bear

If grief is an animal, make it a bear
hibernating cold and hard
in the back-cave of your heart.
In the restlessness of spring,
groggy, hungry, it will rise without warning
gnawing its pain straight through.
There will be no escape
for the soft pulsing of your heart
torn and bled by that bear's sharp incisors.

Grief, the sinner's corsage—
unresolved guilt,
moments which cut like a knife,
then bleed loss across frozen expanses
of forward-time
dancing with shadows from the past.
Memories sharp like razors
slice your disbelief
to emptiness, sullen and alone.
The wind, such cool relief, blows
atoms of loss like snow across a plain.

Some day you will rise above
that bed of sorrow,
the sky so blue and bright
all you can see is white, miracle of sunlight.
That bear, sated in the warmth
will sit amongst ripe berries on high hills,
at peace, at one, at last.

Spring's Last Vespers

I lit a candle for you
in the still sanctuary
that smelled of wood and time.
Outside, a young bird
sang her own praises to the day,
while the traffic noise
pulsed past disjointedly.

And as I sat,
the fading evening light and spring
breeze through the open windows
mingled shadows and curtains,
chorusing into the silence
a stillness for my soul.

Heirloom

Every winter I pull my blue-gray
sweater from the drawer,
slide my arms into the sleeves,
pull the body over my head.

More than thirty years ago,
my mother bought a large bag
of thick wool yarn on sale,
knitting this plain straight sweater,
just for me, every stitch a hug.

Sound of Rain

The sound of rain changes
as leaves appear.
Staccato strike of winter
replaced by brush stroke
of spring. Rebirth is muting
last season's stark hand.

A Bit of Attention

I am reluctant to look forward,
try and catch the end
of the world just beyond the horizon,
until I call to mind each day
the sun comes round pouring forth
love, freely given and eternal.
This is the time of possibility.

I zip my jacket up with satisfaction
against the chill of the forest floor.
I am content to walk alone
amongst the firs—
gray sky, a soothing balm,
indiscernible sound of clouds
sliding overhead,
stillness in the air,
leading my heart to prayer.

Storm Reflections

1.
The wind begins
to pick up, birds
at the feeder hold on.
What do the great cedars feel
as their branches begin to wave?
And the raptors
as they hang
in the dissonance of the breeze?

2.
All day rain,
as if roiling waves
pounding the nearby shore
have risen to the sky.
Bubbling rambling currents
wash ditches deeper.
Great liquid sheets
splash to the ground.

3.
After its exhaustive run
through the night,
the storm abates.
Daylight will dispel our unease,
carrying it away
on a hastening breeze.

April Notes

Rain in the gutters.
April bird-songs.

Be kind, forgiving, gentle
without me.

Sorrow clings
wild and empty
as the sun slowly rises.

Like a stupor—
this waiting for inspiration,
like a decision—
these streaks of clouds.

On Edge

I stand on this edge of cliff
too close for comfort,
so close it feels as though I float
above the driftwood
ready to wing across
the rolling waves.
So close,
I don't trust myself to move.

I whisper the Lummi word
for thank-you—"Hy'sxw'qe"
and imagine these stones
washed and tumbled in the tide
appreciate the sentiment
held in that ancient sound.

Trespass of my ancestors,
who squeezed that language
into small dots upon the map,
interwoven
with my own existence,
this instant poised
on the edge of eternity.

I step forward
toward the quiet saltwater
expanse, this mother ocean
shimmering gray-white
under slate-gray skies.
I find a centeredness
in each bare moment,
my heart in my throat,
sea watering eyes
brimming like waves.

Round the Corner

As I begin my run
cascading sunlight
cuts through cool April air
warms me
even as fine droplets of rain
blown from the squall
far across the valley
tap my face—
pinpricks of moisture.

The wind slips
along my body, breath
heavy—in and out,
a confluence
of atoms and energy
borrowed from the universe.

EVENING

This Year

I have stood in a north wind
so cold it caught my breath
and would not give it back

slept on the expectant
ground of spring, surprised
that winter's chill still lingered there

walked on trails
through forests so dense
I perceived their primordial stillness

and was humbled in the presence
of trees so old
that history barely existed.

I have struggled up rocky slopes
to vistas so wide I felt
I could fly with the gods

yet cowered in the dark
as lightning split the sky into
surreal visions of night and day

and trembled to the cannon
crack of thunder
bolting down the mountainside.

Mystery

Soft rise, fall of mother's breathing,
I cannot sense this motion in the trees.
Soft ebb and flow of tide receding,
what strange emotions such as these?

Memories of comfort in the breath,
limbs stretch upward to the sky.
That which once receded still has left
mysteries surrounding me—but why?

New Year's Eve, 2019

We close another year,
watching that day-lit line
skimming the earth
without surcease.

Arriving on the heels of yesterday,
this day will fade as our future
blossoms on the far horizon.

This sad year filled
with loss and sorrow,
only mystery awaits tomorrow.

Night Cry

An unearthly cry some nights
shivers through the dark.

I like to think it's a bobcat.
But you're sure it's the barred owl
we've seen lately,
odd daylight vision
atop a fence post
or camouflaged in an alder,
robins squawking their displeasure.

High-pitched night cry
lonely, menacing.
A short scale
fanning silence.

Waking Alone In the Mountains

The night is close.
Stars shine through the open tent-fly,
cool wind rustles against pines,
water trickles over jumbled rocks,
shadows dance.

Waking alone in the mountains—
mice and chipmunks scratch,
an owl hoots, beautiful mournful
howl of the coyote.

Waking alone in the mountains
I know my courage and my fright.
They will do battle throughout the night.

Pounding Rain

Pounding rain
stronger than a shower-head
on the rainfly of my tent.

I wait for the evening light to fade,
everything damp, ground hard,
wind so wild I think the tent
might blow away, me inside.

Crash of thunder
up off the cliffs, shaking the clouds,
shaking the air, shaking my unease.

Brilliant flash of lightning,
the world for an instant
bright white and then so dark
I imagine I'll never see again.

To Our Mothers

Are your names hidden in the dark
recesses of our souls
Are your voices what we hear
in the echo of our laughter
Is your touch the weight
that lingers in our hearts
Is your scent a sweetness
wafting on the wind

Are you whispering a lullaby
through the ages
Is your love like the stars
shimmering in the night sky
when the air crackles with the cold
and the light of the bright moon
is flush and full
pregnant with expectation

Did you sit by the river
where we last saw you
one summer evening lost in thought
Did you offer us comfort as we lay awake
at night puzzling out our future path
Did you show us the tendrils
of unconditioned love
Did you give us the power
to understand our place
in the long chain of ancestors

Are your hearts still beating through
DNA of past mothers
into our DNA and into our daughters
Will you sanctify the path
on which we tread
keeping your memories close
as we follow where you led

Death

There is no ordinary anymore.

We sort puzzle pieces across the table
as if we believe setting this scene to rights
could repair our own.

It is solace, and no solace,
just as it should be.

We could not know what was to come,
and yet, it seems we did.

December

"Walk gently, be kind," she said.
"Each ordinary day will pass
with extraordinary speed."

Glistening snow,
drops of white moonlight
tumbling toward earth
leave me exhausted,
wrapped in woolens,
staring out in solitude.
I light a candle to remember
we are a rare piece of magic
in the midnight black.

I saw my long-dead mother
in a dream last night.
We hugged and hugged. I saw in her eyes—
light sparkling as the darkness loomed.

Safe travels, safe homes.
Gratefulness, presence.
Distillation of love and awareness.

Flying East

Just once, flying east across the arctic circle
out the window I saw the edge of night,
hazy darkness against bright sunlight,
heading straight to heaven's sight
we left the world behind.

Standing Naked

Standing naked
in the night's rain,
drops scoring skin
with pinpricks of chill,
raising hairs
in a primitive
useless response
for warmth.

Water
sliding down arms, legs,
soaking in a renewal
you hadn't known was needed.

River

I have risen
to the wash of the river,
a wordless resonance
that sweeps the air
with endless exchange.
It was there as I lay
in the stillness of night,
ushered in my waking,
will persist when I am gone.
It is a song from the world
everlasting, ever changing;
flowing through me always,
through us all, evermore.

When I Wake In the Night

the coyote sings, if I am lucky,
and the spring peepers call
their insistent song of invitation.

When I wake in the night
I discover myself
a mere moment
sprinkled with stars.

Caught Without Their Glory

Zipped into a mountain tent
three hours of daylight left.
Thunder and rain
storm down rock cliffs,
rain-fly snaps in the wet assault.
Alpine meadow solitude.

Just yesterday at 85 degrees
without a breath of wind,
sun-scorched and sweat-sticky,
I longed for the faintest hint
of cloud-shade to pass by.

Tonight above these roiling clouds
Perseid meteors score the sky
with brilliant streaks of wonder.
But the fickleness of circumstance
keeps me caught without their glory.

Tomorrow's sun will burn
all clouds to wisps,
wind and heat will shake
all dampness from the air.
The brilliance of the new day will
chase my evening tedium away.

Fork In the Road

Hecate stands at the fork in the road.
She guides me, if I listen.

I discovered her standing there
last winter, when I was
reading about my deep roots
of womanhood.
I knew she was strong,
a capable guide
who offered strength
and courage through wisdom.

But like the scarecrow
from *The Wizard of Oz*
she pointed one way, then the other,
and in the end
I had to choose
myself.

I could have left my dream—
my dream.
I waited at that fork for months,
wondering if I had the courage,
the fortitude, the strength.

Hecate sat with me there,
quiet and comforting,
helping me weigh my thoughts,

my feelings,
until I was ready to try.

I remember the excitement of beginning,
trying not to invest too much, too soon,
thinking I might turn back
to the ordinary lighted way
of day to day.

But I have not—and this path,
this path is mine.

On My Dying Day

I've sometimes thought
that on my dying day
I'd like to wake one last time
to the song black-capped
chickadees sing at dawn,
welcoming back the sun.

I'd like to listen
while those first rays
slide over the trees
through my window
across my bed.

I'd like to feel
just one last time, that
joy of early morning.

One August Morning

at Cloudy Pass
when the lupines cast a gauze of purple
across the meadows green
filling the air with their heady scent,
when the paintbrush dot the fields like
small red torches beckoning on,
when mouse-on-a-stick raise
their fuzzy heads
a miniature forest above them all,
and the daisies that aren't daisies bloom
with all the white and yellow flowers
whose names I've never learned,
when the sun spreads
her morning welcome
and the trickling stream
splashes mossy stones,
then
then

Turn my ashes free.
It is as it has always been.
It is as it shall be.

Special Thanks…

…to the women in my writing group,
Wildhaven Writers: Amy, Courtney, Katie,
Leslie, and Nancy. Their years of
encouragement and support have been
essential to my development as a poet.

…to my dearest friends, Jana Kay, Laurie,
and Melody, who all in their various ways,
keep me moving forward with my dreams.

…to Steven, husband and best friend,
whose devotion helps me fly.

About the Author

Suzanne Harris is a retired educator, ukulele enthusiast, poet, and writer. Her poetry and prose have been published in *Spindrift; Whatcom Writes!; Women's Bodies, Women's Words;* and several anthologies. She is a 2020 *Sue C. Boynton Poetry Contest* Walk Award recipient and a Merit Award recipient in 2014. Suzanne enjoys living "out in the county" with her husband and loves to play in the North Cascades with her dog, Rizzoli. *Sparks Along the Warp* is her first book of poetry.

www.ingramcontent.com/pod-product-compliance
Lightning Source LLC
Chambersburg PA
CBHW061144160726
48006CB00038B/2242